Revised and Expanded

Peace Primer II

Quotes from
Jewish
Christian
Islamic
Scripture & Tradition

Lynn Gottlieb
Shomer Shalom Network for Jewish Nonviolence

Rabia Terri Harris
Muslim Peace Fellowship

Ken Sehested
Baptist Peace Fellowship of North America

WIPF & STOCK · Eugene, Oregon

Wipf and Stock Publishers
199 W 8th Ave, Suite 3
Eugene, OR 97401

Peace Primer II
Quotes from Jewish, Christian and Islamic Scripture and Tradition
By Gottlieb, Lynn and Harris, Rabia
Copyright©2012 by Gottlieb, Lynn
ISBN 13: 978-1-5326-3176-4
Publication date 4/26/2017
Previously published by Baptist Peace Fellowship of North America, 2012

Meinrad Craighead's prints are repoduced with the permission of
Rowman & Littlefield Publishing Group. They were originally
printed under the title *Liturgical Art*, 1988, Sheed & Ward.

Contents

Introduction

The original *Peace Primer,* compiled and written by Rabia Terri Harris and Ken Sehested, was published in 2002 as a direct result of collaboration between the Baptist Peace Fellowship of North America (BPFNA) and the Muslim Peace Fellowship. It was created as a popular education tool around which members of local churches and mosques could gather for conversation and interfaith bridge-building in the volatile environment following the terrorist attacks of September 11, 2001.

"It is common today to hear the claim that we are engaged in a *clash of cultures,*" in the words of the original document's introduction. "Often, what is meant is a clash between Christian and Muslim cultures."

Multiple printings attest *Peace Primer's* continuing usefulness. Copies circulated as far as Abbottabad, Pakistan, resourcing a Christian-Muslim dialogue. Given the increasing (and hopeful) interfaith conversations among the three "Abrahamic" religious traditions, the BPFNA decided to enlarge the document's scope. Rabia and Ken invited Rabbi Lynn Gottlieb, coordinator of the Shomer Shalom Network for Jewish Nonviolence, to join the editorial team for this revised *Peace Primer II.*

You need not be a professional mediator to know that, frequently, the first step in addressing conflict is for all parties to listen to each other. That is the modest goal of this publication: to allow Jews, Christians and Muslims to listen to each other's Scripture and tradition, particularly to hear what each has to say about seeking justice, pursuing peace and working for reconciliation. (And, for some in each of these faith communities, to be introduced in new ways to their own tradition.)

In the pages to come you will find three sections:

- a general overview of our respective traditions' understandings of "peace" (in the widest, most comprehensive sense of the word);

- a collection of quotations from our scriptures and faith

traditions which speak to the peacemaking mandates of our faith; and

- brief essays from each of us on how we interpret difficult texts.

In addition, there is a joint statement we make together about the purpose, promise and peril of interfaith engagement, as well as suggestions about how to use this document to foster the relationships required for effective collaboration. This, after all, is the point of interfaith dialogue: not simply learned conversation, but making common cause for the justice needed for peace to grow, beginning in our own neighborhoods. Building a *culture of peace* requires people of shared interest and parallel values to negotiate and implement strategies that foster health.

Needless to say, behind these convictions is a lifetime of concrete faith commitments. We readily confess—each of us—that we have come up short more times than we like to admit; that our faith is too often mixed with fear; that we are forever wrestling with the temptation to wield the guidance of our respective traditions for self-interested expedience. Our own personal spiritual formation is ongoing, just as it shapes and is shaped by our public vision, what Dr. Martin Luther King Jr. called the *Beloved Community.*

Lynn Gottlieb, coordinator
Shomer Shalom Network for Jewish Nonviolence

Rabia Terri Harris, founder
Muslim Peace Fellowship

Ken Sehested, founding director
Baptist Peace Fellowship of North America

With this revised edition we offer our special gratitude to the Fellowship of Reconciliation USA, the oldest and largest interfaith peace organization in the US. It was within FOR's orbit that this document's co-editors became acquainted. *(See p. 76 for more information.)*

Jewish Scripture includes the oral and written traditions which evolved over a two thousand year period and are endowed with sacred status. The word "Torah" means "instruction" or "guidance" and refers to both Torah Sheh B'khtav (the written Torah) and Torah Sheh B'al Peh (the oral Torah). The written Torah incorporates the first Five Books of Moses as well as Prophets and Writings. This collection is called TaNaKh, an acronym of these three sections otherwise known as the Bible. Torah and corresponding verses in Prophets and Writings are chanted in synagogue on Sabbath and Holy Days.

The oral Torah refers to the Mishneh and Gemora known collectively as the Talmud, as well as to the body of literature known as Midrash. The Talmud (which also means instruction) interprets the legal material of the written Torah, whereas Midrash represents collections of works focused on the narrative portions of the written Torah. These works are typically studied in schools of Jewish learning. There are hundreds of post-Talmudic commentaries which accompany traditional study, the most famous of which was written by the medieval French sage Shlomo Yitzhaki, known by his acronym "Rashi."

Both the written and oral Torah are considered by rabbinic tradition to have been revealed at Sinai, that is, equally sacred.

They are studied in a way that values multivocalism and majority and minority opinions, as well as linguistic, allegorical, ethical and mystical perspectives.

The Holy Bible, sacred scripture for Christians, is a collection of books written over a period of 10 centuries. All Christians recognize as Scripture what is traditionally known in the church as the Old Testament (sacred to both Jews and Christians and designated here as Hebrew Scripture) and the New Testament. Roman Catholic, Eastern Orthodox, Coptic and Ethiopian Christians also claim divine inspiration for a larger collection commonly referred to as the Apocrypha.

That part of the Bible uniquely honored by Christians is commonly referred to as the New Testament. "Gospel," whose root meaning is "good news," is used broadly to indicate the content of the Christian message. More narrowly, the term designates each of the first four books of the New Testament, containing Jesus' teachings and stories from his life. The remainder of the New Testament, most or all of which was written in the first century C.E., is composed of early church history and pastoral letters authored by various leaders of the early church.

The Qur'an ("The Reading" or "The Recital"), sacred scripture for Muslims, is organized into 114 chapters of varying length. It was revealed through the Prophet Muhammad in the context of many events over the course of the 23 years of his mission. Its text is revered as the direct word of God. The Qur'an makes many direct and indirect references to the Jewish and Christian scriptures.

Muhammad (CE 570-632) is the model of perfect conduct for every Muslim: anecdotes of his life number in the thousands. His transmitted actions and sayings have been categorized and are continuously tested for reliability by succeeding generations of Muslim scholars. This body of reports is called *ahadith* (singular, *hadith*), which literally means "news" but is generally translated as "traditions." Some few sayings were indicated by the Prophet as spoken by God, but not included in the Qur'an: these are known as *ahadith qudsi* or "sacred accounts."

Among the most widely respected compilations of Prophetic traditions are those of Muslim, Bukhari, Tirmidhi, and Abu Dawud, as well as the *ahadith* included in *al-Muwatta* of Imam Malik (all 9th century CE). Highly regarded later works include *Mishkat al-masabih* of Tabrizi (14th c), *al-Jami' as-saghir* of Suyuti (16th c.) and *Kunuz al-haqa'iq* of Munawi (17th c.). All these collections are cited here.

TIKUN OLAM

YOU ARE NOT
OBLIGATED TO
COMPLETE
THE WORK, BUT
NEITHER ARE YOU
FREE TO
ABANDON IT.

רבי טרפון אומר

לא עליך המלאכה לגמור

ולא אתה בן חורין להבטל ממנה.

אם למדת תורה הרבה

נותנים לך שכר הרבה

ונאמן הוא בעל מלאכתך

שישלם לך שכר בעולתך

10

Shmirat Shalom
A Contemporary Expression of Jewish Nonviolence

Jewish tradition is crafted around a system of ethical and ritual behaviors called *mitzvot*. *Mitzvot* are meant to promote restorative justice and peace while discouraging violence. *Shmirat Shalom*, or nonviolent peace stewardship, is the practice of this system based on the principles of nonviolence found within the tradition as well as contemporary anti-oppression work. Judaism is a deed-oriented system rather than a belief-oriented system. For this reason, Judaism has developed a system of practice known as *halakha* or walking on the Way.

The following *middot*, or guiding principles, represent the foundational principles of *Shmirat Shalom*. They are drawn from both the Written and Oral traditions of Torah.

1. **YHVH Ekhad** *(Deuteronomy 6:7)*. Life is sacred and inter-related. (Jewish people do not pronounce the ineffable Name.) When we recite the biblical prayer *Shema Yisrael*, "Listen Israel . . . YHVH is one!" the intention is to honor the oneness of all life. If we are all interconnected, then every action we take either heals or harms the great web of being. Judaism teaches us to be awake to the sacredness of all living beings as the first step on a spiritual pathway.

2. **Love your neighbor as you love yourself** *(Leviticus 19:18)*. Do not do to others that which is hateful to you *(BT Shabbat 31a)*. The commandment to love your neighbor is amplified by the instruction to cause no harm. Both are considered foundational to all of Torah. As Baal Shem Tov taught us, "Love your neighbor. Why? Because every human being has a root in the Unity. When you harm one aspect, you harm the whole." Loving others is a

way to love the Creator. Love is revealed in deeds of compassion and, on occasion, acts of restraint.

3. **Great is human dignity** *(BT Berakhot 19b).* Our tradition teaches that human dignity—*kavod ha-adam*—trumps all other obligations. Pious observance cannot offset actions that compromise human dignity. The sages taught, "A person should be concerned more that he or she not injure others than that he or she not be injured." Each face mirrors a divine reflection to be cherished. Righteousness occurs when dignity is preserved in our interactions with fellow humans and creatures that share planet earth.

4. **Pursue justice, truth and peace. Justice and truth lead to peace.** It is written, "By three things the world is preserved, by [restorative] justice, by truth, and by peace, and these three are one: if [restorative] justice has been accomplished, so has truth, and so has peace" *(JT Ta'anit 4:2).* The voice of the prophets insist on the relationship between justice, truth and peace. Speaking truth to power is urgent. Addressing oppression involves understanding the way we profit from it. Repairing the wounds of injustice requires transforming underlying social conditions.

5. **Practice teshuvah** [reconciliation]. The goal of conflict transformation is not to defeat the enemy, but to transform the conditions that produce injustice. *Teshuvah* is a response to injustice that involves taking responsibility for one's deeds (confession) along with an acknowledgment of the collective accountability for injustice. Only then can we successfully engage healing, forgiveness and restoration. *Teshuvah* involves everyone impacted

by injustice to be involved in the healing process.

6. **"Do not envy a person of violence**. Do not choose any of his [violent] ways" *(Proverbs 3:31)*. Violence is a response that causes intentional harm, or passive participation in systems of harm. Violence is considered *muktzeh* [forbidden] by a person who practices *shmirat shalom* or Jewish peace stewardship. That is, we are prohibited from engaging in acts that harm. Therefore, we must continually re-examine our beliefs and actions to make sure they are *kosher* [fit for use] in the religious practice of *shmirat shalom*.

7. **"Not by military might**, and not by force of arms. By spirit [nonviolence] alone, says Adonai" *(Zechariah 4:6)*. Therefore, refuse to cooperate with oppression and nonviolently resist structural violence. This principle requires Jews who follow the path of *shmirat shalom* to refrain from participating in war or occupation. It is an act of both noncooperation and constructive peace building.

8. **"Seek shalom and pursue it"** *(Psalm 34:15)*.
   Seek shalom for your loved ones and pursue it for your enemies.
   Seek shalom where you live and pursue it elsewhere.
   Seek shalom with your body and pursue it with your material resources.
   Seek shalom for yourself and pursue it for others.
   Seek shalom today and pursue it every tomorrow.
   (Vayikra Rabbah 9.9)

Lynn Gottlieb

Fritz Eichenberg, "The Peaceable Kingdom"

The Bible Speaks About Peace
Twelve Things Every Christian Should Know

Peace is the will of God. From the first chapter of Scripture, where God pronounced creation "good" *(Genesis 1:31)*, to the very last, in John's vision of a tree "for the healing of the nations" *(Revelation 22:2)*, God pursues peace. Trust in God is frequently contrasted with trust in the instruments of war *(Isaiah 31:1; Psalm 20:7, 33:16-17; Hosea 1:7)*.

Peace was the mission of Jesus. Jesus' role as "the Prince of Peace" was foretold by Isaiah *(9:6)*. Angles announcing the birth declared "Glory to God" and "peace on earth" *(Luke 2:14)*. Weeping over Jerusalem Jesus prayed: "would that you knew the things that make for peace" *(Luke19:41-42)*.

The fruit of the Spirit is peace *(Galatians 5:22)*. "Not by might, nor by power, but by my spirit, says the Lord" *(Zechariah 6:4)*. Prior to his death, Jesus said, "Peace I leave with you," in reference to the coming presence of the Holy Spirit *(John 14:25-27)*.

Peace was the witness of the early church. The new community created in Christ bore witness by its reconciled fellowship: "And all who believed were together and had all things in common" *(Acts 2:44-47; 4:32-37)*. Paul urged that the church's "feet" be "shod with the gospel of peace" *(Ephesians 6:15)*.

Peace is more than the absence of war. Peace—*shalom*—occurs when captives are released *(Luke 4:18)*; when outcasts are gathered

(Zephaniah 3:19); when the hungry have plenty to eat *(Joel 2:19-26; Luke 1:53; 1 Samuel 2:1-8)*.

The foundation of peace is justice. "The effect of righteousness [justice] will be peace," predicted Isaiah *(32:17)*. "Righteousness and peace will kiss each other," wrote the psalmist (86:10). "Sowing justice" will result in peace, wrote Hosea *(10:12-14)*.

Peace, like war, is waged. Peacemakers are not passive, but active. Peter, echoing the psalmist, urges us to "seek peace, and pursue it" *(1 Peter 3:11; Psalm 34:14)*. Jesus urged worshipers to take the initiative to settle disputes *(Matthew 5:23-24)*. Peace includes loving and feeding enemies *(Luke 6:27; Romans 12:20)*.

Peacemakers sometimes cause trouble. Jesus turned over the tables of oppressive money-changers *(John 2:13-16)*. When he says, "I come not to bring peace but division *(Luke 12:51)*, the "peace" of which he speaks merely disguises an order of injustice *(cf. Jeremiah 6:13-15)*. It was Jesus' peacemaking mission which landed him on the cross *(Colossians 1:20)*.

Peacemaking is rooted in grace. In Jesus' prayer, our "debts" are forgiven in the measure by which we forgive others *(Matthew 6:12)*. "Whoever is forgiven little, loves little" *(Luke 7:47)*. It is grace which frees us from fear *(1 John 4:18)* and empowers us to risk our lives for justice and peace.

Peace in Christ and peace in creation are linked. Not only are divisions in the human community overcome "in Christ" *(Galatians 3:28)*, but also in the whole created order. The knowledge of God and the healing of creation are parallel realities *(Isaiah 11:3-9)*. The land itself mourns *(Isaiah 33:9)*. "But ask the beasts…and the birds…or the plants, and they will teach you" of the ways of the Lord *(Job 12:7-10)*.

Peacemaking is not optional for the church. The separation between "preaching the Gospel" and "working for peace and justice" is a perversion of biblical truth. Jesus prayed: "Thy kingdom come, thy will be done, on earth as it is in heaven" *(Matthew 6:10)*. We lie if we say we love God yet fail to assist neighbors in need *(1 John 4:20)*. Loving enemies—whether close at hand or far away—is the way to become children of God *(Matthew 5:44-45)*.

God's promised future is peace. Though now living as "aliens" in a strange land, peacemakers have caught a glimpse of how the future will finally unfold. Both Isaiah and John's Revelation speak of the coming "new heaven and new earth" *(Isaiah 65:17-22; Revelation 21:1)*. The day is coming, says Micah, when nations "shall beat their swords into ploughshares…and neither shall they learn war any more" *(4:3-4)*. On that day, creation itself, which "has been groaning in travail . . . will be set free from its bondage to decay" *(Romans 8:19-24)*.

Ken Sehested

In the Name of God All-Compassionate, Most Merciful

Points of Guidance for Muslim Peacemakers Taken from the Generous Qur'an

Remember God first, above all, and throughout the process of peacemaking. No peace can be established without an awareness of God.

Will not God defend His servant? Yet they would frighten you with others beside God. Whomever God sends astray, for him there is no guide. Whomever God guides, for him there can be no misleader. Is not God Mighty, Able to Requite [the wrong]? And indeed, if you should ask them: Who created the heavens and the earth? They will say, God. Say: Think about the ones you serve beside God. If God willed some hurt for me, could they remove from me His hurt; or if He willed some mercy for me, could they restrain His mercy? Say: God is enough for me. In Him do the trusting put their trust. Say: O my people! Act in your manner: I too am acting.

Surah Zumar, 36-39

Try to draw all parties into a common frame of understanding.

Say: O people of the Book! Come to common terms as between us and you: that we worship none but God; that we associate no partners with Him; that we do not set up from among ourselves Lords and patrons other than God. If then they turn back, say: Bear witness that we [at least] are *muslim* [embracing God's will].

Surah Al'Imran, 64

Never cease to remember that all acts have consequences.

Do then those who devise evil feel secure that God will not cause the earth to swallow them up or that the wrath will not seize them from directions they little perceive? Or that He may not call them to account in the midst of their goings to and fro without a chance of their frustrating Him? Or that He may not call them to account by a process of slow wastage? For your Lord is indeed full of kindness and mercy.

Surah Nahl, 45-47

Strive for justice. It isn't easy.

O you who believe! Stand out firmly for justice as witnesses to God even as against yourselves or your parents or your kin and whether rich or poor: for God can best protect both. Follow not the lusts [of your hearts] lest you swerve, and if you distort or decline to do justice, indeed God is well-acquainted with all that you do.

Surah Nisa', 135

Help contestants to clarify their principles, and hold them to the principles they profess. This is not easy either.

To each among you We have prescribed a Law and an Open Way. If God had so willed He would have made you all one community but [He wishes] to test you in that which He has given you, so compete with each other in good works. The goal of you all is God; it is He that will show you the truth of the matters in which you dispute.

Surah Ma'idah, 48

Ease the hearts of the oppressed.

The recompense of an ill deed is the like thereof. But whosoever pardons and amends, his reward is due from God, who does not love tyrants.

Surah Shura, 40

Respect the human dignity of the opponent.

O you who believe! Be steadfast witnesses for God in equity, and let not hatred of any people seduce you that you deal not justly. Deal justly: that is nearer to consciousness of God. Be conscious of God; indeed God is aware of what you do.

Surah Ma'idah, 8

Lift up the generosity of God.

What can God gain by your punishment if you are grateful and keep faith?

Surah Nisa', 147

The good deed and the evil deed are not alike.

Repel evil with that which is better, then he between whom and you there was enmity will become like an intimate friend. But none is granted it save those who are steadfast, and none is granted it save the holder of great happiness.

Ha Mim, 34-35

Rabia Terri Harris

Editors' note: Hebrew Scripture refers to the Pentateuch, Prophets and Writings. Both Jewish and Christian believers consider the material sacred. Christians traditionally refer to this collection as the Old Testament. At least 50 figures mentioned in the Bible are also mentioned in the Qur'an. For more information on Jewish terminology, see p. 7.

Jewish Scripture

When a person lets his livestock loose to graze in another's land, and so allows a field or vineyard to be grazed bare, he must make restitution for the impairment of that field or vineyard.

Exodus 22:4

Do not follow the majority to do evil.

Exodus 23:2

A stranger you shall not harm, neither shall you violently oppress, for you are no strangers to oppression. The stranger who resides with you shall be to you as one of your citizens; you shall love him as yourself, for you were strangers in the land of Mitzrayim.

Leviticus 19:33-34, Exodus 22:20

You shall have one law for stranger and citizen alike.

Leviticus 24:22

When you build a new house, make a fence for your roof lest someone fall off the roof.

Deuteronomy 22:8

Do not pervert justice for the stranger or the orphan, do not take a widow's garment as security for a loan. You must remember that you were enslaved in Egypt.

Deuteronomy 24:17-18

I call heaven and earth to witness before you on this very day, behold life and death, blessing and curse. Choose life, so both you and your descendants live.

Deuteronomy 30:19

A king is not saved by his great army; a warrior is not delivered by his great strength. The war horse is a vain hope for victory, and by its great might it cannot save.

Psalm 33:16-17

Some boast of chariots and some of horses but we boast of the name of YH. YY's delight is not in the strength of horses, Nor does YH find pleasure in the legs of a man. Rather YH takes pleasure in those who hope in YH's steadfast love.

Psalm 147:10-11

If a person returns evil for good, evil will not depart from her house.

Proverbs 17:13

Then justice will dwell in the wilderness, and righteousness abide in the fruitful field. And the effect of righteousness will be peace. . . .

Isaiah 32:16-17

Cry out with a full throat, without restraint. Make your voice a shofar! You pray fervently and then complain, "Why wasn't my prayer answered?" You repeat ancient pieties in the sanctuary of the Lord, yet you seem not to know. On this, your day of fasting, you oppress your laborers. You stand guard on a continent named injustice that burns bodies to the bone. You piously berate each other about misdeeds, confess guilt, and then beat down the poor with a violent fist. Is this the fast acceptable in a house of peace? Is this the fast Adonai has chosen? Let your fast be the deeds that break the grip of oppression. Let your supplications be the hand that removes the yoke of unethical action from around your neck. Rise up from the pew and shake the foundations of exploitation. Let the imprisoned and detained go free. Break the habit of consumerism. Give fresh bread

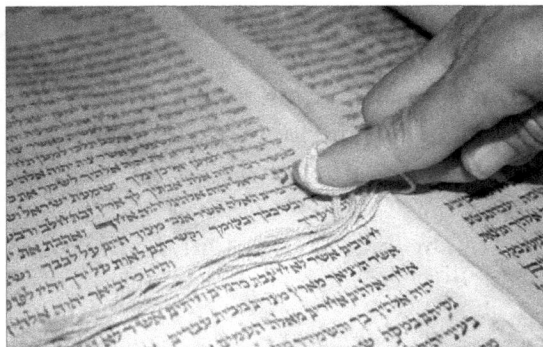

to the hungry. Bring the poor you cast naked into the street into your house and home, and do not hold back but extend a helping hand to the human family and all life on earth. Then shall your inner light break forth, radiant as the light of dawn.

Isaiah 58:1-10 (RLG translation)

He judged the cause of the poor and needy; then it was well. Is not this to know me? Says the Lord.

Jeremiah 22:16

I have no pleasure in the death of the wicked, but that the wicked turn from his way and live.

Ezekiel 33:11

But I will have pity on the house of Judah, and I will deliver them by the Lord their God; I will not deliver them by bow, nor by sword, nor by war, nor by horses, nor by horsemen.

Hosea 1:7

Because you have trusted in your power, and in the multitude of your warriors; therefore the tumult of war shall rise among your people.

Hosea 10:13b-14

What does the Lord require of you but to do justice, and to love kindness, and to walk humbly with your God.

Micah 6:8

They shall beat their swords into plowshares, and their spears into pruning hooks; nation shall not lift up sword against nation, neither shall they learn war any more.

Micah 4:3

Woe to the one who piles up what is not his. Woe to the one who has acquired gains to the detriment of his house...for a stone will cry out from the wall, and a rafter shall answer it from the woodwork. Woe to him who builds a town with blood, and founds a city on iniquity.

Habakkuk 2:9-12

Not by military might, and not by force of arms. Only by My spirit.

Zechariah 4:6

Jewish Tradition

YHVH is the completeness of everything.

Tikkunei HaZohar 17b

The verse, "One human being was created" teaches you that a person who kills another human being, kills an entire world, and kills all future generations that would have been born from that soul. The verse "one humanity was created" teaches you: A person who saves the life of just one person, saves an entire world, saves all future generations born from that single soul.

Sanhedrin, 37a (This verse also appears in Qur'an.)

There is no person who is insignificant and no thing improbable. There is no person that does not have their hour and no thing that does not have its place.

Pirkei Avot 4:3

When you harm one aspect you harm the whole.

The Baal Shem Tov

When the Spirit of Life created the first human, YHVH took the human before all the trees of the garden. "See my works, how fine and excellent they are. All I have created has been given to you. Remember this and do not corrupt and desolate my world, for if you corrupt it, who will come after you to set it aright."

Ecclesiastes Rabbah7

A person should be concerned more that he not injure others than that he not be injured.

Tosefta to Baba Kama 23b

R. Simeon B. Abba said: Not only a person who returns evil for good, but even a person who returns evil for evil, evil will not depart from one's house.

Beresheet Rabbah 38:3

Diana Bryer, "Rabi Lynn"

I bring heaven and earth to witness: The Holy Spirit dwells upon a non-Jew as well as upon a Jew, upon a woman as well as a man, upon a maid and man servant as well as their employer. All depend upon the deeds of the particular individual.

Tanna de Veit Eliahu

It has been further been taught: "It is forbidden to sell them weapons or accessories to weapons, nor should one sharpen weapons for them. One may not sell them blocks or neck bands placed on prisoners or ropes or iron chains, neither to idolaters [*Romans] nor to Cuthites [a sect of Judaism]. R. Nahman said in the name of Rabbah b. Avuha: Just as they ruled that it forbidden to sell [these items] to an idolater so is it forbidden to them to an Israelite who is suspected of selling them to an idolater. The rabbis taught: It is forbidden to sell them shields [used for decorative purposes], but others say that shields may be sold to them. Said R. Nahman in the name of Rabba b. Avuha: The law agrees with the others.

Yerushalmi 15b-16a

[Implicit in the reference to "idolaters" are Roman gladiators, forced to fight to the death as a form of entertainment, as well as Rome's imperial occupation.]

The pious of all nations have a place in the world to come.

Sanhedrin 105a/Babylonian Talmud

When our masters entered the vineyard at Yavneh, (that is, when they sat in formal session, they like rows of vines in a vineyard) among them were R. Judah, R. Yose, R. Nehemiah and R. Eliezer the son of R. Yose the Galilean. In appreciation of the hospitality shown them, they began their discourse by expounding texts on hospitality. "You shall not abhor an Edomite, for he is your brother; you shall not abhor an Egyptian because you were strangers in his land."

Beresheet Rabbah 63b

A peace that comes from fear and not from the heart is the opposite of peace.

Gersonides

Alexandri said, Two donkey drivers who hated each other happened to walk alongside each other on the road. One of their donkeys sat down under the pressure of its load. His companion saw it and passed on. When he passed he thought: It is written in the Torah, "If you see the donkey of one who hates you, you shall surely help him lift it up." Immediately he returned and helped his companion with the load. He, the former, began to say to himself: So and so is my friend and I did not know. Both entered an inn and ate and drank together. Who is responsible for their making peace? The fact that the latter had looked into the Torah, accordingly it is written: You have established righteousness.

Midrash Tanhuma on Psalm 99:4

Eye for an eye was never intended to mean equal retribution. Rather it means monetary compensation for damages. When one person injures another, the Talmud tells us this person is "liable to pay the costs of the others' healing."

Mishna Baba Kamma 8:1

When two men were in a conflict, Aaron would go and sit with one of them. He would say to him: My son, look at your friend, [look at what he is saying], he is tearing at his heart and ripping his clothing. He says, 'Woe is me, how can I lift my eyes and see my friend. I am ashamed before him, for it is I who wronged him. And he [Aaron] would stay with him until he removed all of the jealous rage from his heart. And Aaron would then go to the other man, and say [the same thing]. And when the two would finally meet, they would hug and kiss each other.

Pirkei Avot 1:12

Rabbi Joshua ben Korha taught: Where there is strict justice there is no peace; where there is peace, there is no strict justice. He consequently instructed the judge,"act as an arbiter," that is, rule for compromise, which is justice tempered with peace.

Jerusalem Talmud Sanhedrin 1:5; Sanhedrin 6b

Once an arrow leaves the bow, not even the strongest warrior can bring it back.

Avot de Rebbe Natan, 2nd century Israel during Roman occupation

Whoever is able to protest against the transgressions of his own family and does not do so is held responsible and liable for the transgressions of his family. Whoever is able to protest against the transgressions of the people of his community and does not do so is liable for the transgressions of his community. Whoever is able to protest against the transgressions of the entire world and does not do so is liable for the transgressions of the entire world.

Babylonian Talmud Shabbat 54b

How long should one continue to resist injustice? One hundred times, even though the first 99 are disregarded. We are also urged to protest until we swing the balance of the scales to the side of merit.

Talmudic tractate Chagigah 9b

Who is the greatest hero? One who changes an enemy into a friend.

Avot de Rebbe Natan 23

If a person of learning sits in his or her home and says to herself, "What have the affairs of society to do with me? Why should I trouble myself with the people's voices of protest? Let my soul dwell in Peace!" If he does this, he overthrows [destroys] the world.

Tanhuma Mishpatim

In Gen. 37:3-4 when [Joseph's] brothers saw that their father loved him more than any of his brothers they hated him so much, they could not speak a friendly word to him [they could not speak a single word of peace to him]. On the other hand, if the brothers had sat in council, and spoken, each person to their brother [or sister], and talked it through with each other, bringing up the wounding, they could have reconciled with each other. The trouble is, in every conflict there is not a mutual language nor a balanced understanding [between parties]. If there is no effort to restore relationships by sitting and talking it through as described above, then contentiousness will remain.

Hasidic

The sword comes into the world for the delay of justice and for the perversion of justice.

Pirkei Avot 5:11

Through what means do we blot out Amalek [hated enemies] and through what means do we blot out those who glorify the sword? How, and in what manner are we to bring an end to the world's militarism? The view of Judaism is: evil cannot be extirpated by evil means, terror cannot be eliminated through the use of counter-terror. Therefore, one cannot destroy a "strong arm" with a "strong arm," and one cannot obliterate a sword with a sword. And when Judaism declares a war against militarism, it cannot declare it through militarism. About this it is said: "Write this in a book of remembrance," that is to say: "wage war against the sword with the book."

*Moshe Avigdor Amiel, Chief Rabbi of Tel Aviv
from 1936-46, Derashot el Ami 3, p. 132*

A Jewish court of sages which executed one person in seven years was called a murderous court. "One in seventy years," says Rabbi Elazar ben Azariah.

Mishna Makkot 1:10

If your enemy is hungry, even though he rose early to kill you and came hungry and thirsty to your home, feed him and give him to drink.

Rabbi Hama bar Hanina

For when a man tries to keep watch that his fist not injure others, by that very act he enthrones in the world the God of truth and righteousness and adds power to the kingdom of justice; it is precisely this power which will defend him against injury by others.

Aaron Samuel Tamaret, quoted by Everett Gendler,
"Therefore Choose Life," in Roots of Jewish Nonviolence,
edited by Murray Polner, Stefan Merken and Alan Solomonow

I refuse, after all, to be loyal to a policy of humiliation, racism and discrimination. I am neither loyal to the settlers nor to house demolitions. I cannot be loyal to the silencing of opposition and to the oppression of the needy and destitute. I am not loyal to the blockade on Gaza and the expulsion of Palestinian residents in Jerusalem. And certainly, I am unwilling to be loyal to the killing of children.

Neve Gorden, "No Citizenship Without Loyalty," in
Midnight on the Mavi Marmara: The attack on the Gaza
Freedom Flotilla and how it changed the course of the
Israeli-Palestinian Conflict, *edited by Moustafa Baymoui*

Meinrad Craighead, "Menorah"

Editors' note: See pp. 23-26 for a list of texts from Hebrew Scripture, also honored as sacred by Christians.

Christian New Testament

Blessed are the peacemakers, for they shall be called children of God.

Matthew 5:9

You have heard that it was said, "An eye for an eye, and a tooth for a tooth." But I say to you, Do not resist an evildoer. But if anyone strikes you on the right cheek, turn the other also. . . . You have heard that it was said, "You shall love your neighbor and hate your enemy." But I say unto you, Love your enemies and pray for those who persecute you.

Matthew 5:38-39, 43-44

Then Jesus said to [Peter]: "Put your sword back into its place; for all who take the sword will perish by the sword."

Matthew 26:52

[God] has put down the mighty from their thrones . . . and exalted those of low degree; he has filled the hungry with good things, and sent the rich away empty.

Luke 1:51, 52b-53

The Spirit of the Lord is upon me, because he has anointed me to preach good news to the poor. He has sent me to proclaim release to the captives and recovering of sight to the blind, to set at liberty those who are oppressed, to proclaim the acceptable year of the Lord.

Luke 4:18-19

If you love those who love you, what credit is that to you? For even sinners love those who love them. And if you do good to those who do good to you, what credit is that to you? For even sinners do the same. And if you lend to those from whom you hope to receive, what credit is that to you? Even sinners lend to sinners, to receive as much again. But love your enemies, and do good, and lend, expecting nothing in return; . . . and you will be children of the Most High.

Luke 6:32-35

A new commandment I give unto you, that you love one another; even as I have loved you, that you also love one another. By this everyone will know that you are my disciples.

John 13:34-35a

Repay no one evil for evil. . . . Beloved, never avenge yourselves, but leave it to the wrath of God. . . . If your enemies are hungry, feed them. . . . Do not be overcome by evil, but overcome evil with good.

Romans 12:17a, 19a, 20a, 21

See that none of you repays evil for evil, but always seek to do good to one another.

1 Thessalonians 5:15

What causes wars, and what causes fightings among you? Is it not your passions that are at war in your members? You desire and do not have; so you kill. And you covet and cannot obtain; so you fight and wage war.

James 4:1-2

All who hate a brother or sister are murderers. . . . Those who say, "I love God," and hate their brothers or sisters, are liars.

1 John 3:15a; 4:20a

Then I saw a new heaven and a new earth; for the first heaven and the first earth had passed away. . . . And I heard a loud voice saying, "See, the home of God is among mortals. [God] will wipe away every tear from their eyes, and death shall be no more, neither shall there be mourning nor crying nor pain any more, for the former things have passed away."

Revelation 21:1, 3a, 4

Christian Tradition

I am a soldier of Christ; it is not lawful for me to fight.

St. Martin of Tours (c.335–397)

Christians no longer take up the sword against nation, nor do we learn war any more, having become children of peace, for the sake of Jesus, who is our leader.

Origen, (c.185–254)

When Christ disarmed Peter in the garden, he disarmed all Christians.

Tertullian (c.160–c.225)

Twelve men went out from Jerusalem into the world, and they were ignorant men, unable to speak; but by the power of God they told every race of men that they were sent by Christ to teach all men the word of God. And we who formerly slew one another not only do not make war against our enemies, but for the sake of not telling lies or deceiving those who examine us, gladly die confessing Christ.

St. Justin, Martyr (in a letter describing the Christian movement to the Roman Emperor, c.150)

Now the trumpet sounds with a mighty voice calling the soldiers of the world to arms, announcing war. And shall not Christ, who has uttered his summons to peace even to the ends of the earth, summon together his own soldiers of peace? Indeed, O Man, he has called to arms with his Blood and his Word an army that sheds no blood. To these soldiers he has handed over the Kingdom of Heaven. . . . Let us be armed for peace, putting on the armor of justice, seizing the shield of salvation, and sharpening the "sword of the spirit which is the Word of God" (Eph. 6:13-17). This is how the Apostle [Paul] prepares us for battle. Such are the arms that make us invulnerable.

Clement of Alexandria (c.150–c.215)

Acquire the spirit of peace and a thousand souls around you will be saved.

St. Seraphim of Sarov (1759–1833)

A soldier under authority shall not kill a man. If he is ordered to, he shall not carry out the order; nor shall he take the oath. If he is unwilling, let him be rejected. He who has the power of the sword, or is a magistrate of a city who wears the purple, let him cease or be rejected. Catechumens or believers who want to become soldiers should be rejected, because they have despised God.

Apostolic Tradition, 16 (Rome, early 3rd century)

If anyone be a soldier or in authority, let him be taught not to op-press or to kill or to rob, or to be angry or to rage and afflict anyone. But let those rations suffice him which are given to him. But if they wish to be baptized in the Lord, let them cease from military service or from the [post of] authority. And if not let them not be received.

Testamentum Domini, 2.2 (Asia Minor, mid-4th century)

Of the magistrate and soldier: let them not kill anyone, even if they receive the order to do so. Let them not put crowns on. Anyone who has authority and does not do the justice of the gospel, let him be cut off and not pray with the bishop.

Canons of Hippolytus, 13–14 (Egypt, mid-4th century)

Imagine the vanity of thinking that your enemy can do you more damage than your enmity.

St. Augustine (354–430)

It is certainly a finer and more wonderful thing to change the mind of enemies and bring them to another way of thinking than to kill them, especially when we recall that the [disciples] were only twelve and the whole world was full of wolves. . . . We ought then to be ashamed of ourselves, we who act so very differently and rush like wolves upon our foes. So long as we are sheep we have the victory; but if we are like wolves we are beaten, for then the help of the shepherd is withdrawn from us, for he feeds sheep not wolves. . . .

This mystery [of the Eucharist] requires that we should be innocent not only of violence but of all enmity, however slight, for it is the mystery of peace.

St. John Chrysostom (c.347–407)

Lord, make me an instrument of thy peace. Where there is hatred, let me sow love; where there is injury, pardon; where there is doubt, faith; where there is despair, hope; where there is darkness, light; where there is sadness, joy.

Prayer of St. Francis of Assisi (1181–1226)

Meinrad Craighead, "I Was Hungry" cf. Matthew 25:31-45

True evangelical faith cannot lie dormant. It clothes the naked; it feeds the hungry; it shelters the destitute; it serves those that harm it; it binds up that which is wounded. It has become all things to all.

Menno Simons (c. 1496–1561),
after whom Mennonites are named

And they being the redeemed of the Lord, who dwell in the house of the Lord, upon the Mount Sion, do change their fleshly weapons, namely, their swords into [plow]shares, and their spears into scythes, do lift up no sword, neither hath nor consent to fleshly battle.

John Smyth, considered the co-founder in 1610
of the first Baptist congregation

No Baptist will be found in war, and few in prison or on the gallows because of their crimes. The majority of them are inclined to peacefulness. . . . It would be desirable that the whole world were full of these "deteriorated" Baptists. . . . May God keep all Baptists in His grace so that they may not turn toward evil once more and then their outcome will be as mentioned above, namely the eternal life of joy.

18th century German Baptist pastor Alexander Mack

That Your Petitioners are wholly adverse to the custom and practice of War, believing it to be a combination of the greatest of crimes and on the largest scale; and that they consider [a military spending proposal] as tending to disturb the peace of the world [and] to provoke the aggression which it proposes to prevent.

Peace petition sent in 1860 by the Mill Yard
Seventh Day Baptist Church, London, to the British Parliament

I repent of whatever expressions or acts in my past life may have cherished the war spirit. I repent that I have so long delayed to enter my protest against the practice of war [which is] the indispensable duty of every Christian.

Adoniram Judson, pioneering Baptist missionary (1788–1850)

Peace Primer II

Meinrad Craighead, "The Earth Rejoices," cf. Revelation 21:5

May we look upon our treasures, the furniture of our houses and our garments and [judge] whether the seeds of war have nourishment in these our possessions.

John Woolman (1720–1772)

The great crime of war can never promote the religion of peace. The battle and the garment rolled in blood are not a fitting prelude to "peace on earth; goodwill to men." And I do firmly hold that the slaughter of men, that bayonets, and swords and guns, have never yet been, and never can be promoters of the Gospel.

Charles Haddon Spurgeon, renowned
19th century British Baptist pastor

[A] nation cannot wage war to the glory of God. The doctrine of the cross, self-giving, self-suffering, forgiveness, is the exact opposite of the doctrine of armies and navies. One must choose between the sword and the cross.

Muriel Lester, founder of Kingsley Hall, London (1883–1968)

Do we really believe that Christianity will perish unless it be defended by war? . . . If we do believe that, then we have deliberately passed a vote of no confidence in Christianity. If Christianity needs this kind of defence then there is little that is really divine about it. . . . We must conclude that a faith which needs the defence of modern warfare is not a faith which even deserves to survive.

William Barclay, Scottish New Testament scholar (1907–1978)

Peace plans its strategy and encircles the enemy. Peace marshals its forces and storms the gates. Peace gathers its weapons and pierces the defense. Peace, like war, is waged. But Christ has turned it all around: the weapons of peace are love, joy, goodness, longsuffering; the arms of peace are justice, truth, patience, prayer; the strategy of peace brings safety, welfare, happiness; the forces of peace are the sons and daughters of God.

Walker Knight, Baptist editor

President Jimmy Carter quotes these lines in his speech sealing the Camp David Accords, signed by Egyptian President Anwar El Sadat and Israeli Prime Minister Menachem, on 17 September 1978

Peacemaking is not an optional commitment; it is a requirement of our faith. We are called to be peacemakers, not by some movement of the moment, but by our Lord Jesus.

"The Challenge of Peace," U.S. Catholic Bishops (1983)

Peace is not the product of terror or fear. Peace is not the silence of cemeteries. Peace is not the result of violent repression. Peace is generosity; it is right and duty.

Archbishop Oscar A. Romero, martyred in El Salvador, 1980

When the economy is geared to the arming of the heavens rather than the development of the heart, neighbors and nations must learn to cry out their dissatisfaction together.

Joan Chittister, OSB

Concern for peace, whether Jewish or Christian, is part of the purpose of God for all eternity. God is by nature a reconciler, a maker of shalom. For us to participate in the peacemaking purposes of that kind of God is not just morality. It is not just politics. It is worship, doxology, praise.

John Howard Yoder

A nation that continues year after year to spend more money on military defense than on programs of social uplift, is approaching spiritual death.

Dr. Martin Luther King Jr., civil rights leader

We want to bathe in the blood of the dragon and drink from the blood of the Lamb at the same time. But the truth is that we have to choose.

Dorothee Sölle, German theologian

The prophetic understanding of God as warrior is rooted in the liberating act of God in the exodus. Because *God* is warrior, Moses—the archetypal prophet—instructs the people that it is not up to them to fight. "And Moses said to the people, 'Fear not, stand firm, and see the salvation of the Lord, which he will work for you today. . . . The Lord will fight for you, and you have only to be still'" (Exodus 14:13-14).

A Declaration On Peace: In God's People the World's Renewal Has Begun (1991), Douglas Gwyn, George Hunsinger, Eugene F. Roop, John Howard Yoder

A church that is not able to take a firm stand against war is not a church which deserves to be believed.

Harvey Cox

On the edge of this new millennium we testify to the Spirit's plea to the church and to the world: Disarm your hearts! Repent of your habits of violence and injustice; return to the One who bore you in mercy; rebuild ruined neighborhoods; restore marginalized peoples; resume the politics of forgiveness and an economy of manna *[sufficiency]*; revive an ecological relationship with the created order; reject the escalating culture of violence and renew your commitment to building a culture of peace.

"Open Letter to the 18th Baptist World Congress," International Baptist Peace Conference, January 2000, Melbourne, Australia

Disarming the Heart
The gospel of nonviolence

Editor's Introduction: Parentheses indicate source citations. All sources are standard references for reliable reports. It is customary to invoke blessings upon the Prophet every time his name is mentioned. I have spelled this out initially, then abbreviated later occurrences with the symbol (s), standing for salawat, or blessings.

God Almighty and Glorious says: O My servants, I have forbidden oppression for Myself and have made it forbidden among you, so do not oppress one another. O My servants, all of you are straying save those I have guided, so seek guidance of Me and I shall guide you. O My servants, all of you are hungry save those I have fed, so seek food of Me and I shall feed you. O My servants, all of you are naked save those I have clothed, so seek clothing of Me and I shall clothe you. O My servants, you sin by night and by day, and I forgive all sins, so seek forgiveness of Me and I shall forgive you. O My servants, you will not attain to harming Me so as to harm Me, and will not attain to helping Me so as to help Me. O My servants, were the first of you and the last of you, the humans among you and the genies among you to be as pious as the most pious heart of any single person among you, that would not increase My kingdom in anything. O My servants, were the first of you and the last of you, the humans among you and the genies among you to be as wicked as the most wicked heart of any single person among you, that would not decrease My kingdom in anything. O My servants, were the first of you and the last of you, the humans among you and the genies among you to rise up in one place and make a request of Me, and were I to give all what they requested, that would not decrease what I have, any more than a needle tossed into the sea decreases the sea. O My servants, it is only your own deeds that I reckon up for you and then recompense you for, so let whoever who finds good praise God, and let whoever finds other than good blame no one but himself.

Hadith Qudsi

The Messenger of God (peace and blessings be upon him) said: When God created the creation, He inscribed upon the Throne, "My Mercy overpowers My wrath."

Bukhari and Muslim

Attributed to Jesus (peace be upon him): Do not speak much without the mention of God for you will harden your hearts. A hard heart is far from God, but you do not know. Do not look at the wrong actions of other people as if you were lords. Look at your own wrong actions as if you were servants. Some people are afflicted by wrong action and some people are protected from it. Be merciful to the people of affliction and praise God for His protection.

al-Muwatta

The Messenger of God (s) sent Mu'adh [as a governor] to Yemen and said, "Be afraid of the curse of the oppressed, for there is no screen between their prayer and God."

Bukhari

The Messenger of God (s) said: One who supports an oppressor and strengthens him, knowing that he is an oppressor, has gone out of Islam.

Mishkat al-masabih

The Messenger of God (s) said: "Do you know who is destitute?" They [the Companions of the Prophet] said: "A destitute man among us is one who has neither money nor property." He [the Prophet] said: "The destitute man of my community is the one who will come on the Day of Resurrection with prayers and fasts and obligatory charity, but since he hurled abuses upon others and brought calumny against others, unlawfully consumed the wealth of others and shed the blood of others and beat others, his virtues will all be credited to the account of others. And if his good deeds fall too short to clear his account, then those others' sins will be entered into it and he will be thrown into Hell."

Muslim

The Messenger of God (s) said: That man whose neighbor is not safe from harassment has no faith.

Bukhari and Muslim

The Messenger of God (s) said: Whoever is untrustworthy in his dealings has no faith, and whoever is not committed to his promises has no religion.

Bayhaqi

A funeral procession passed by the Messenger of God(s), and he said, "One is relieved, while another, others are relieved from!" They said, "Who is the one relieved and the one from whom others are relieved?" He said, "A faithful servant is the one who is relieved from the exhaustion and the suffering of this world by the mercy of God, and an unjust servant is the one from whom people, towns, trees, and animals are relieved."

al-Muwatta

The Messenger of God (s) said: The best servants of God are those who, when they are seen, cause God to be remembered. The worst servants of God are those who go about slandering, who separate friends and seek to distress the upright.

Tirmidhi

The Messenger of God (s) said: It does not befit a faithful person to have a full belly while his neighbor goes without.

Bukhari and Muslim

The Messenger of God (s) said: Anything kept with [the Muslims] in trust should be safely returned, and if anyone has misappropriated their property, they should not misappropriate his in return.

Mishkat al-masabih

The Messenger of God (s) said: When you hear a man say, "The people are ruined," he himself is the most ruined of them all.

al-Muwatta

When the Prophet rode by [a place called] al-Hijr, he said, Do not enter the house of those who were unjust to themselves, unless [you enter] weeping, lest you should suffer the same punishment as was inflicted upon them." And he covered his face with his saddlecloth.

Bukhari

The Messenger of God (s) said: "Help your fellow Muslim whether oppressor or oppressed." "We know how to help the oppressed, but how are we to help the oppressor?" "Your help to him is to prevent him from oppressing."

Bukhari

A man came to the Prophet(s) and said, "Messenger of God, teach me some words that I can live by. Do not make them too much for me, lest I forget." The Messenger of God said, "Do not be angry."

al-Muwatta

The Messenger of God (s) said: A strong person is not the person who throws his adversaries to the ground. A strong person is the one who contains himself when he is angry.

al-Muwatta

The Messenger of God (s) said: God informed Prophet Moses (peace be upon him) that of all His servants, the dearest to Him was he who was strong enough to take revenge and yet forgives.

Mishkat al-masabih; Bayhaqi

The Messenger of God (s) said: The doors of Paradise are opened each Monday and Thursday. Every submitting servant who does not associate anything with God is forgiven except for the one who is at enmity with his brother. It is said, "Leave these two until they have reconciled. Leave these two until they have reconciled."

al-Muwatta

The Prophet mentioned the Fire and sought refuge with God from it, and turned his face aside. He mentioned the Fire again and took refuge from it and turned his face aside. Then he said, "Save yourselves from the Fire even if with one half of a date fruit [given in charity], and if this is not available, then by saying a good pleasant friendly word."

Bukhari

The Messenger of God (s) said: A believer is friendly.

Tirmidhi

The Messenger of God (s) said: The best friend in the sight of God is the well-wisher of his companions, and the best neighbor is the one who behaves best toward his neighbors.

Tirmidhi

The Messenger of God (s) said: Beware of suspicion. Suspicion is the most untrue speech. Do not spy and do not eavesdrop. Do not compete with each other and do not envy each other and do not hate each other and do not shun each other. Be servants of God, brothers.

al-Muwatta

The Messenger of God (s) said: Equanimity, gentleness, and good behavior are one twenty-fifth of prophethood.

al-Muwatta

The Messenger of God (s) said: Moderation is the best course of action.

al-Jami'al-saghir, Konuz al-haqa'iq

The Messenger of God (s) said: God has mercy upon those who are merciful to others.

Bukari

The Messenger of God (s) said: You cannot be admitted to Paradise and cannot be truly faithful until you have affection for one another.

Muslim

The Messenger of God (s) said: Shake hands and rancor will disappear. Give presents to each other and love each other and enmity will disappear.

Al-Muwatta

The Messenger of God (s) said: Every act of kindness is charity, and kindness includes meeting your brother with a cheerful face and pouring water from your bucket into your brother's vessel.

Tirmidhi

"In the name of God, Most Gracious, Most Merciful."

The Messenger of God (s) said: The cure for hard-heartedness is to put an affectionate hand on the head of orphans and to feed the poor.

Mishkat al-masabih

Mu'adh ibn Jabal (may God be pleased with him) reported: Rejoice! For I heard The Messenger of God (s) say "God, the Blessed and Exalted, said, 'My love is due to those who love each other in Me, and those who sit with each other in Me, and those who visit each other in Me, and those who give to each other generously in Me.'"

al-Muwatta

The Messenger of God (s) said: The warrior is the one who battles with his own self on the path of God.

al-Jami' al-saghir, Konuz al-haqa'iq

The Messenger of God (s) inquired about a milk camel ready to be milked. "Who will milk this camel?" he asked. A man stood up. The Messenger of God asked, "What is your name?" The man said, "Murrah [bitterness]." The Messenger of God said to him, "Sit down." Then he said, "Who will milk this camel?" A man stood up and the Messenger of God asked, "What is your name?" He said "Harb [war]." The Messenger of God said, "Sit down." Again he said, "Who will milk this camel?" A man stood up, and the Messenger of God asked, "What is your name?" The man said, "Ya'ish [he thrives]," The Messenger of God said, "Milk!"

Al-Muwatta

Wathilah b al-Asqa' (may God be pleased with him) reported: I asked, "Messenger of God, does a man's love of his people indicate tribal partisanship?" He replied, "No, but when a man helps his people in wrongdoing it indicates tribal partisanship."

Tirmidhi and Abu Dawud

The Messenger of God (s) said: One who is killed under the banner of a man who is blind, who raises the slogan of family or supports his own tribe, dies the death of one belonging to the days of Ignorance.

Muslim

The Messenger of God (s) said: If any ruler having authority over Muslim subjects dies while he is deceiving them, God will forbid him Paradise.

Bukhari

Abu Dharr (may God be pleased with him) reported, The Messenger of God (s) said to me, "What will you do, Abu Dharr, when you see the Ahjar az-Zayt covered with blood?" I replied: "What God and His Messenger choose for me." He said: "You must go to those who are like-minded." I asked: "Should I not take my sword and put it on my shoulder?" He replied: "You would then associate yourself with the people." I then asked: "What do you order me to do?" "You must stay at home." I asked: "And if people enter my house and find me?" He replied: "If you are afraid the gleam of the sword may dazzle you, put the end of your garment over your face in order that [the one who kills you] may bear the punishment of your sins and his."

Abu Dawud

The Messenger of God (s) said: If a man abuses and shames you for something which he finds in you, then do not shame him for something which you find in him; he will bear the evil consequences for it.

Abu Dawud

Khabbabah (may God be pleased with him) reported: We complained to The Messenger of God (s) [of the persecution inflicted on us] while he was sitting in the shade of the Ka'bah. We said to him, "Would you seek help for us? Would you pray to God for us?" He said, "Among the nations before you a [believing] man would be put in a ditch that was dug for him, and a saw would be put over his head and he would be cut into two pieces; yet that [torture] would not make him give up his religion. His body would be combed with iron combs that would remove his flesh from the bones and nerves, yet that would not make him abandon his religion. By God, this religion will prevail till a traveler from Sana [in Yemen] to Hadramaut will fear none but God, or a wolf as regards his sheep, but you people are hasty."

Bukhari

The Messenger of God (s) said: Whoever has forbearance, God will help him. Whoever tries to be independent of people, God will enrich him. Whoever tries to be patient, God will give him patience, and no one is given a better or broader gift than patience.

al-Muwatta

The Messenger of God (s) said: God says, "I have nothing to give but Paradise as a reward to my faithful servant, who, if I cause his dear one to die, remains patient."

Bukhari

The Messenger of God (s) said: No one will suffer any bodily injury and forgive it without God raising him a degree for it and removing a sin from him.

Tirmidhi

The Messenger of God (s) said: Do not long to engage your enemy, but ask God for safety.

Bukhari

The Messenger of God (s) said: The spirits are like armies arranged in ranks. Those who have recognized one another in this world will become friends, and those who have not recognized each other will be in conflict.

Muslim, Bukhari, and al-Jami' al-saghir

The Messenger of God (s) said: All people belong to God's family, and God favors best those who are most useful to His family.

al-Jami' al-saghir, Konuz al-haqa'iq

The Messenger of God (s) said: The best jihad is to speak a word of truth to an unjust ruler.

Abu Dawud

Abu Dharr (may God be pleased with him) reported: My friend ordered me to observe seven things. He ordered me to love the poor and be near them; he ordered me to consider my inferior and not consider my superior; he ordered me to join ties of relationship even when relatives were at a distance; he ordered me not to ask anyone for anything; he ordered me to speak the truth even when it was bitter; he ordered me not to fear for God's sake reproach anyone may cast on me; and he ordered me to repeat often "There is no might and no power except in God," for these words were part of the treasure under the Throne.

Tirmidhi

The Messenger of God (s) used to supplicate God: "My Lord, help me and do not give help against me; grant me success, and do not grant success against me; plan on my behalf and do not plan against me. Guide me, and make my right guidance easy for me; grant me victory over those who act wrongfully toward me. O God, make me grateful to You, mindful of You, full of awe toward You, devoted to Your obedience, humble before You, and penitent. My Lord, accept my repentance, wash away my sin, answer my supplication, clearly establish my evidence, guide my heart, make true my tongue, and draw out malice from my breast."

Abu Dawud

Umm Salamah (may God be pleased with her) reported: The Messenger of God (s) never went out of my house without raising his eyes to the sky and saying: "O God! I seek refuge in You lest I stray or am led astray, slip or am made to slip, cause injustice or suffer injustice, do wrong or have wrong done to me."

Abu Dawud

The Messenger of God (s) said: There is a reward for serving any living thing.

Bukhari

The Messenger of God (s) said: There are people among the servants of God who are neither prophets nor martyrs; the prophets and martyrs will envy them on the Day of Resurrection for their rank before God, the Most High." People asked: "Tell us, Messenger of God, who are they?" He replied: "They are people who love one another for the spirit of God, without any mutual kinship or exchange of property. I swear by God, their faces will glow and they will stand in light. They will have no fear when the people will fear, and they will not grieve when the people will grieve." He then recited the Qur'anic verse: "Behold! Verily for the friends of God there is no fear, nor shall they grieve."

Abu Dawud

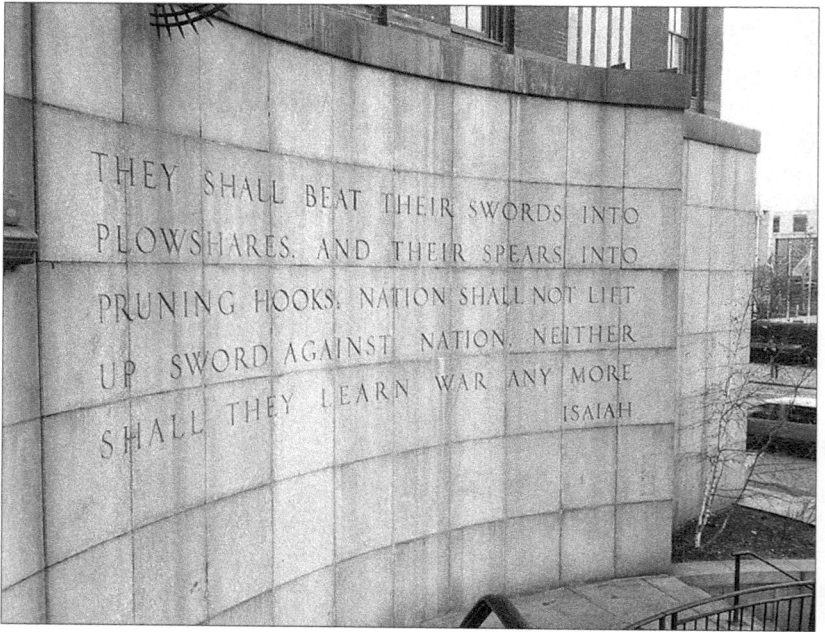

"Isaiah Wall," Ralph Bunche Park, across from the United Nations, New York, NY (cf. Isaiah 2:4)

Interpreting a Torah of Nonviolence

Although there are many acts of violence in the Written Torah, the rabbinic sages that developed the Oral Torah created a series of strategies that altogether eliminated or severely circumscribed the application of these passages to the real world. The process of curtailing the application of biblical laws that promote violence led to the evolution of rabbinic Judaism's preference for nonviolence as a way of life. Rabbinic Judaism rarely honors warriors. Rather, classical Judaism shows a preference for the wisdom of sages committed to study, community service and prayer, and views violence as *muktzeh*, something which should be avoided altogether. The following limited examples illustrate rabbinic Judaism's preference for nonviolence.

While the Written Torah contains the famous passages that instructs "an eye for an eye," the rabbinic sages never interpret this literally. Rather, they understand "an eye for an eye" to mean equivalent monetary compensation. Regarding the instruction to stone to death a rebellious child, the sages comment that stoning one's son to death was never applied. "It never happened and never will happen!" They simply could not image a moral universe which permitted this kind of behavior sanctioned by Torah.

Even in response to the genocidal passages that contain God's command to kill all the Moabites, the Torah offers a counter narrative that seems to contradict the command. Ruth is a Moabite woman whose kindness is celebrated as a model for the kind of godly behavior that exemplifies the message of Torah. Thus, the rabbinic sages assigned the reading of the Scroll of Ruth the Moabite to Shavuot, the holy day that celebrates the giving of the Torah. Talmudic sages reinforce lenient attitudes toward non-Jews and acknowledge the presence of the righteous among all peoples.

There are hundreds of such examples that amount to a trend in rabbinic literature favoring nonviolence and expressing distain for violence. They call anyone who lifts a hand against another person a *rasha* or evil person. Hillel's famous phrase, "Do not do unto others that which is hateful to you. That is the entire Torah. Now go study," is a foundational principal of Jewish nonviolence. A *shomeret shalom* believes that the Torah must never be used to cause harm. Rather, everything in Torah must prevent harm and cultivate peace.

Nonetheless, some people use Jewish scriptures, both oral and written, to promote violence. If one is an angry person, one will find an angry Torah. If one is a compassionate person, one will find a compassionate Torah. Therefore, as the Torah teaches us, we must choose life and not death, a blessing and not a curse. How best do we choose life? People committed to *shmirat shalom* as a way of life believe that by choosing nonviolence we fulfill the obligation to choose life.

Lynn Gottlieb

I HAVE SET
BEFORE YOU
LIFE AND DEATH
BLESSING AND CURSE
THEREFORE
CHOOSE
LIFE

DEUTERONOMY 30:19

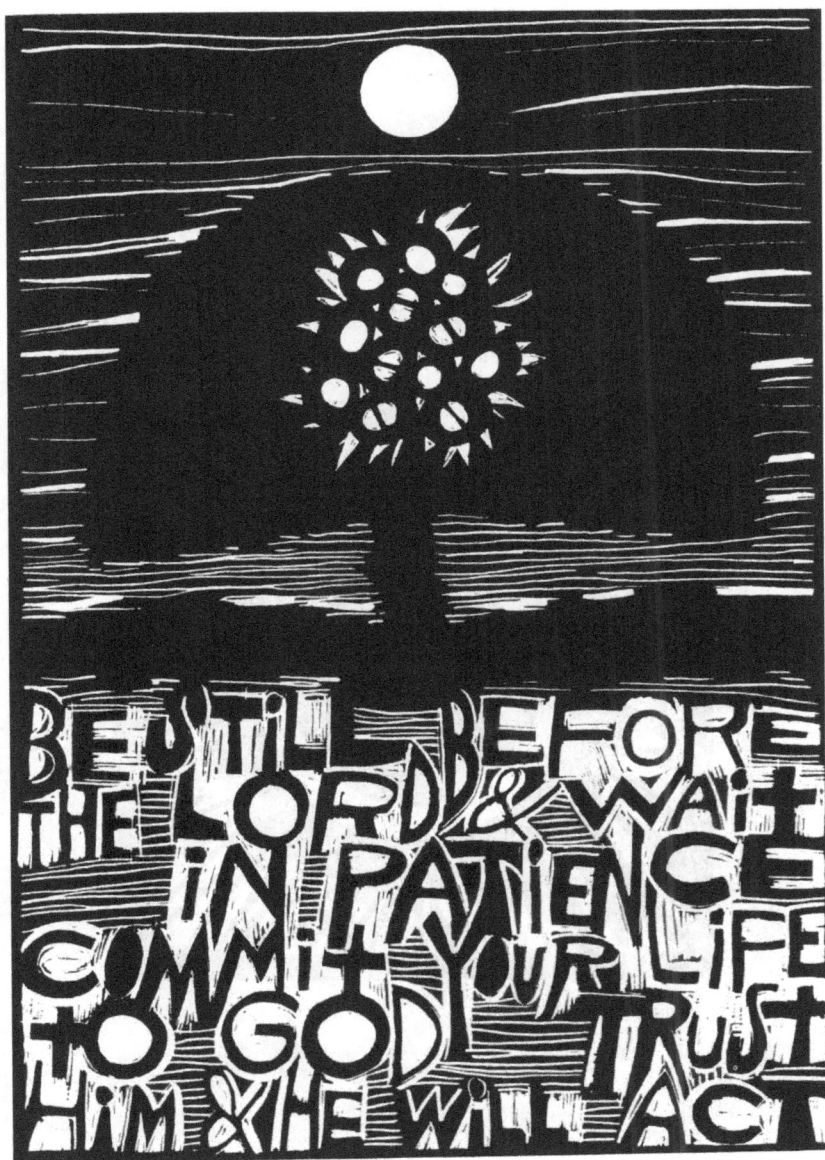

Meinrad Craighead, "Be Still," cf. Psalm 37:7

Meinrad Craigheadd, "Redemption"

Interpreting a Bible of Nonviolence

In response to seeing an early draft of this document, one of my friends wrote: "One of my rabbi friends has pushed me to see it is not enough to just talk about the resources for peace present in religion. There are texts in most religions used to justify war. We need to find ways of acknowledging these texts as well and work with our communities in addressing the presence of both."

He is right, of course. It is not enough, but it is a start. For our modest purpose, we want to introduce Jews, Christians and Muslims to unfamiliar peacemaking streams in each other's traditions (and, in some cases, in their own).

The question, however, remains. Are there violent and vengeful texts in the Torah? In the Qur'an? In the Holy Bible? Some say yes; others say no, only violent and vengeful readings of those texts. Rev. William Sloan Coffin, known for his sharp wit, wrote: "The Bible is a mirror with true reflection. If an ass looks in, don't expect an apostle to look back."

Whatever the case may be, the three of us who collaborated on this book agree that it will not do to simply ignore such contentious texts. Nor should we U.S. Christians ignore our own bitter history of home-grown terrorism, most obviously in the Ku Klux Klan, an organization for whom the cross was its defining symbol.*

How we Christians affirm fidelity to our founding documents while also asserting the centrality of our peacemaking vocation is no simple task. Although I claim no original conclusions, let me briefly mention three provisions guiding my thinking.

Firstly, the root of my convictions, however fallible, is the lived experience of grace. The deeper I experience God's forgiveness, the more forgiving I am of others. In translation, that means my own impulses to violence, whether merely verbal or explicitly physical, are diminishing. Grace is not a private experience designed to make you feel good now and get you into heaven later. Grace is a fear-displacement process whose ultimate goal is the overthrow of a world warped by malice and wounded by enmity.

Secondly, while the "holy war" tradition in Christian scripture presents a clear dilemma for those committed to nonviolence, advocates of redemptive violence consistently overlook the most distinctive element of these narratives: the promise that *God* will do the fighting, i.e., that victory comes not from human strength, calculation or technology.

The military strategy of Moses, engineering the Hebrews' Egyptian prison break; or of Gideon, forced to dramatically reduce the ranks of his army prior to victory; or of Joshua's defeat of Jericho using loud horns and human shouts; or of the lad David, wielding only a slingshot, confronting the weapons-laden Goliath—all such accounts betray any biblical warrant for a "strong national defense." In a stern rebuke to his followers on the night of his arrest, Jesus impeached their violent impulse, saying *don't you know I could call forth legions of battle-ready angels on my behalf?* (Matthew 26:52-53)

Thirdly, it's been said that numbers don't lie, but accountants do. All particular texts must be read in the light of the whole. Some of us within the Christian tribe believe that principles of interpretation ("hermeneutics" is the scholarly word) cannot be located in ecclesial authority, nor simply in the text itself. Rather, "rightly dividing the word of truth" (2 Timothy 2:15) is done within the believing community which is *on the road*, following Jesus, in the context of concrete and risky struggles to be readers *and* doers of the Word of God.

We also believe that Scripture discloses the nonviolent power of God. Our Christian-speak is to acclaim Jesus as the unveiling of God's unilaterally disarming initiative sufficient to provoke the fulfillment of God's original intention in creation, declaring: *it is good* (cf. Genesis 1). Such boasting in the Gospel entails no special merit (cf. Genesis 1). Such boasting in the Gospel entails no special merit of God's mercy. Such mercy is ours neither to hoard nor dispense. We are not its border guards. All are immigrants to that Bright Land into whose citizenship we are invited, for whose establishment we are committed, by whose joyful refrain our tongues cannot be restrained.

That a conflict is underway is not in doubt; and we are enjoined to the struggle. But under different terms.

Ken Sehested

* *James Cone's book,* The Cross and the Lynching Tree, *examines this history and its theological meaning. Philip Jenkins'* Laying Down the Sword: Why We Can't Ignore the Bible's Violent Verses, *exhaustively documents its subject.*

Cross of shell casings, collected by Ken Sehested in Bethlehem near the Church of the Nativity, West Bank.

السلام عليكم

As-salamu alaykum • peace be unto you

Interpreting a Qur'an of Nonviolence

Jihad does not mean "holy war." It means "struggle." The word can imply any sort of effort necessary to secure the welfare of a community of faith, from pursuing scholarship to taking care of widows and orphans. In a famous anecdote, the Holy Prophet told a weary party of soldiers, "You are now returning from the lesser jihad to the greater jihad." "O Messenger of God," they asked, "who are we going to face now?" He replied, "Yourselves."

But there is no question that jihad is frequently used to refer to war: the Prophet so used it himself. He used it in order to impose clear limits upon conflict. One of those limits was the strict protection of noncombatants. Another was the refusal to hate.

Muhammad (peace and blessings be upon him) engaged in the full range of human activity. He got married; he had children; he had business affairs. For part of his life, he made war. Qur'an was revealed in all the changing conditions through which he and his community passed from the time of his calling at age 40 until the time of his passing at 63. The way he lived demonstrated what the divine commandments meant.

Muslims acknowledge that our behavior must be bound by Qur'anic revelation and by Prophetic example, which reaches us through transmitted reports. In all things we refer ourselves to texts. Texts, though, can be read in different ways. In the midst of civil war in the early post-Prophetic community, the fierce opponents of the great spiritual and political leader 'Ali summoned him to negotiations on the basis of the Book of God. He went; but his comment was, "That to which they call me is words on paper. It needs interpreters, and interpreters are people." No matter how much we might wish it otherwise, there is no removing *ourselves* from the process of divine guidance. The insights we are granted ultimately depend on our own faculty of conscience.

Yet while conscience is necessary, it is not sufficient. Growth in understanding comes from conversations among conscience, revelation, and holy example. When being is at its proper point of balance, the three agree. When it is not, they don't. Souls "become" through questions—questions addressed, via our texts, to God.

We all share a commitment to peace. But when Muslims examine what is incompatible in Christian pacifism, we discover two difficulties. One is the teaching "Resist not evil," which leads to the position that fighting is bad. The other is the belief that killing a human being is the worst thing a person can possibly do. Yet the Qur'an clearly tells Muslims that we are called to resist evil, and that fighting is ordained for us, although we may not like it. And while it advises us that saving a single life is of a value comparable to saving the entire world, it also tells us that persecution is even graver than killing.

Many Muslims say, in all sincerity, "I loathe fighting and could never bring myself to kill anyone." However, a coherent Islamic moral argument cannot be formed in this way. Instead, we must accept the ethical priorities enjoined upon us and carefully consider what they entail today.

The first 13 years of the Prophet's mission were devoted to unarmed struggle against oppression. The transition in his last decade to armed resistance occurred only after divine permission. This permission is embodied in Surah Hajj, 39-41:

God defends the faithful. Indeed God does not like every ungrateful betrayer. Permission is given to those who fight because they have been tyrannized, and God is fully able to help them—those who are expelled from their homes without any just claim save that they say, God is our sustainer. Were it not that God drives back the people, some by means of others, cloisters, churches, synagogues, and mosques, wherein God's name is much remembered, would have been pulled down. God will surely help whoever helps Him, for God is strong, indomitable—those who, if we establish them securely in the earth, engage in worship, pay the poor rate, enjoin the right, and oppose the wrong. To God belong the consequences of affairs.

The permission is accompanied by a promise, and contingent upon a covenant, namely to "help God" by conserving the three great dimensions of human responsibility—spiritual ("worship"), social ("poor rate"), and moral ("enjoin and oppose")—upon which all true religion is built. So the lawful struggle of the Muslims is the struggle for the freedom to practice religion. For though the fight of the early community was directly for the safety of its own practice, indirectly it was a fight for the safety of all—"cloisters, churches, synagogues" as well as mosques. Indeed, on the basis of these verses one must hold it unconscionable that Muslims do not routinely rush to the defense of threatened communities of every faith. *"So fight on until there is no more persecution, and religion belongs wholly to God."* (Surah Anfal, 39)

This kind of fight could not be a capitulation to self-interest. The Holy Prophet said, on more than one occasion, "He is not of us who proclaims the cause of tribal partisanship; and he is not of us who fights in the cause of tribal partisanship; and he is not of us who dies for the sake of tribal partisanship." Neither could it involve vindictiveness or revenge. At every point, the behavior of the Prophet's forces was held to standards higher than those of the opposition. In social conflicts as in all of life, the Muslims were to manifest *"something better"* (Surah Anfal, 70). And that is because the object of the Prophet's jihad was not to destroy his enemies, but to win them over.

If we cease to think of nonviolence as a way of avoiding struggle, and begin to think of it as a means of engaging in struggle, we will come to see it clearly as a perfect instrument of jihad. And if we honor the Prophet's rulings on the behavior of combatants, we may conclude that it is presently the *only* valid instrument of jihad.

Rabia Terri Harris

Speak Out Clearly, Pay Up Personally

In the early weeks of 2011, during the Arab Spring uprising, Egyptian blogger Nevine Zaki posted a photograph from Cairo's Tahrir Square. It showed a group of people bowing in the traditional style of Muslim prayer, surrounded by other people standing hand-in-hand, facing outward, as a wall of protection against hostile pro-government forces. Zaki affixed this caption: "A picture I took yesterday of Christians protecting Muslims during their prayers."

Similar scenes—some ancient, some as recent as yesterday's newspaper—have been arranged in a host of ways with a variety of religious identities. No religious tradition can claim a monopoly on compassionate courage. And yet such snapshots remain rare.

Photo by Nevine Zaki

A recent magazine ad for a large U.S. stock brokerage firm features a stunning photograph of the Earth taken from space. Superimposed over that image is the phrase "WORLD PEACE IS GOOD." And then the ad continues: "But finding a stock at 5 that goes to 200 is better." This glimpse of cynicism gives us some idea of the economic and emotional forces we're up against when we try to work for genuine peace.

If the effort to foster understanding and relationships across religious lines is to be more than a cosmopolitan hobby, if it is to become a substantial and sustainable movement, expanding the base is essential. New and renewed strategies and resources are important, as is provoking the kind of imagination that will support costly action. Both these goals require clarifying the purpose and promise, as well as the peril, of interfaith engagement.

This revised and expanded version of *Peace Primer* is being offered in the conviction that interfaith dialogue and collaboration are both possible and urgent. Much has already occurred, and we celebrate, remember and support those inspired individuals and organizations that have led the way. Solidarity in human dignity across apparent boundaries of separation has long been practiced by many people of conscience, in many times and places, though the phenomenon has rarely been afforded the public attention we believe it deserves. Still, plenty of documentation exists.

The purpose of interfaith conversation is not to have exotic friends or engage in literate conversation at dinner parties. The purpose of crossing these boundaries is to affirm the God of Creation, the God of Humanity, in the face of rampant efforts to debase both creation and humanity—efforts that are generally defended with reference to some divinized "greater good." Far too often, such efforts seek to bolster themselves with religious legitimacy of some kind. Coalitions of religious adherents of every sort are therefore needed to mount resistance to the "myth of redemptive violence," as theologian Walter Wink called it—that most enduring of human miscalculations.

The French novelist and journalist Albert Camus was speaking to a group of Christians when he said it, but the audience contains us all: "What the world expects" is that "you should speak out loud and clear . . . in such a way that never a doubt, never the slightest doubt, could arise in the heart of the simplest person. [You] should get away from all abstractions and confront the bloodstained face history has taken on today. We need a group of people resolved to speak out clearly and to pay up personally."

Besides saying *no* to religiously sanctioned violence, multi-faith groups also need to say *yes* to the policies of justice that prepare the ground for a harvest of peace, by means of institutions that serve the *common* good rather than the "greater good." Such policies are forged in the very heart of religious faith. Only a politics of forgiveness and human dignity has the power to free the future from being determined by the failures of the past, to make space for hope.

Conflict mediation specialist Byron Bland has written that two truths make healthy community difficult: that the past cannot be undone, and that the future cannot be controlled. However, two counterforces are available to address these destructive tendencies: the practice of forgiveness, which has the power to change the logic of the past; and covenant-making, which creates islands of stability and reliability in a faithless, sometimes ruthless world. A third counterforce also calls out to be deployed: the exhilaration of our discovery of the usefulness of human difference.

Religious communities have unique resources to foster politically realistic alternatives to policies of vengeance and to shape civic discourse in ways that free communities and nations from cycles of violence. When faith communities actively acknowledge one another's gifts, the whole is far greater than the sum of its parts.

This acknowledgement is essential. For in addition to the purpose and promise of interfaith engagement, there is also a peril that must be avoided. Interfaith dialogue too often presumes that for progress to be made, distinctive faith claims must be abolished, distinctive practices muted. Part of the shadow side of modernism is its tendency to reduce everything to common denominators.

There is a kind of cultural imperialism in this purported "universalism." Interfaith advocates have a tendency to become culture vultures, picking a little from this tradition, a little from that— whatever looks and feels good at the time. Severed from particular

disciplines, historic memory and communal commitments, this kind of freeze-dried spirituality offers sugary nutrition that stimulates but does not and cannot sustain healthy institutions. Politically speaking, the result of this intellectual fickleness isolates progressives from traditional cultures of faith and from the very communities whose collective weight must be brought to bear on our wanton, promiscuous state of affairs, where vulgar enthusiasm for personal gain forever seems to trump the commonwealth.

It has been said that in a drought-stricken land it does little good to dig many shallow wells. We believe that the way forward for interfaith engagement will acknowledge at the outset that energizing interreligious collaboration does not mean homogenizing faith. Of course, that does not mean we shall remain unchanged. But we will be pushed to trust that the Center of our adoration, however that reality is named, is greater than the limits of our comprehension.

In the end, such delight and joy—some say reverence—is the only power that will sustain the risks to be endured.

Rabbi Lynn Gottlieb
Chaplain Rabia Terri Harris
Rev. Ken Sehested

However much you study, you cannot know without action.
—Saadi of Shiraz, Persian poet born in the late 12th century

Dear friends of interfaith dialogue:

We encourage you to read these principles as the first step in interfaith dialogue. The purpose of reading and sharing these principles is to establish a common understanding and agreement of how to conduct a dialogue. The following principles are a suggestion. You can create your own common understanding and agreements, which can be reassessed at any time.

It is important to create an atmosphere of safety and trust among the people who are gathered to learn about each other's faith traditions. Perhaps, you will also decide to share your personal faith stories before you begin a formal study of the *Peace Primer* so that your story becomes part of the conversation. We encourage you to speak as individuals and not feel like you have to represent your entire faith community.

No doubt, your circle of study will include people from different cultural as well as faith traditions. People have different styles of communication and there is a tendency for some people to speak up and others to remain quiet. Using a circle format, which allows each person to speak for a similar amount of time, helps groups promote the voices of everyone present as equal partners in the dialogue.

- Our interfaith work is based on **building multi-faith, intergenerational and multi-cultural relationships** that contribute to the prevention and dismantling of various forms of structural violence and promoting a culture of interfaith understanding and peace. We accept a **universal application of human rights** that affirms the dignity and well-being of every human being, regardless of beliefs.

- In the work of the *Peace Primer* dialogue, we lift up those aspects of Jewish, Christian and Muslim traditions that promote nonviolent conflict transformation, prophetic witness, restorative justice and community peacemaking. We cherish our scriptural traditions.

- We **support non-cooperation** with expressions of state and communally sanctioned violence.

- We recognize that **healing from trauma** by survivors of gender, racial, religious and political violence, whether in the context of their own faith groups, or at the hands of others, must be acknowledged as part of our collective interfaith work. We are sensitive to the personal experiences of suffering and loss in any given group of people.

- As interfaith allies, we are committed to a **truthful examination** of attitudes, beliefs and behaviors in our own traditions that may contribute to sustaining structural violence. However, we are not here to challenge the faith of others in negative ways, but to seek understanding from a place of humility and genuine interest. No one person can represent the whole of a faith community, nor can one person be held responsible for the actions of other members of a faith community. We acknowledge the diversity among faiths and within our faith communities.

- Dialogue participants have chosen aspects of their religious tradition that they feel comfortable sharing in this context, but **dialogue is not an invitation to take or use other people's traditional ways for one's own purposes**. In honoring each other we respect the dignity and right of peoples not to share certain aspects of their tradition and to hold them sacred unto their own community.

- We work for the **well-being and safety** of families and communities throughout the world.

One of the most important things you can do in your local community is to begin developing relationships with the "other"—in this case, among Jews, Christians and Muslims.

Crossing interfaith boundaries is never easy. Going into unfamiliar places, being with unfamiliar people, always takes courage. It may take repeated efforts—don't give up quickly.

Don't try to mask your particular religious identity. Be who you are and respect others for who they are. Searching for common ground does not erase differences.

Some practical suggestions:

- Take initiatives to build bridges among Jewish, Christian and Muslim communities in your area. Suggest this book as an initial agenda for conversation and dialogue.

- Use this book for educational forums in your worshipping community, in faith-based peace and justice organizations, in community centers, in classrooms of various sorts.

- Whenever you come across discriminatory statements by political, religious or community leaders, send them a letter along with a copy of this book.

- Make sure your young people have access to this material. Arrange for them to worship with communities of faith very different from your own. Raising a new generation with wider awareness to diversity is crucial.

- Religious leaders: Circulate this book among your colleagues.

- Prior to major religious festivals and occasions, invite your Jewish, Christian and/or Muslim friends to your place of worship for a meal and educational presentation on the upcoming holy days.

- The purpose of this book is specifically to encourage relationships among Jews, Christians and Muslims. Dialogue between "people of the book" or among the major "Abrahamic faiths" is a great way to begin interfaith dialogue. Use the experience to then cross the boundary with other religious traditions as well.

Artwork by Jody Richards, used with permission. The text is an adaptation by Satish Kumar of a mantra from the Hindu Upanishads and is commonly referred to as the "World Peace Prayer."

Lynn Gottlieb

Rabbi Lynn Gottlieb, author of *She Who Dwells Within: A Feminist Vision of Renewed Judaism*, is coordinator of Shomer Shalom Network for Jewish Nonviolence in Berkeley, California. She is one of the first 8 women to become a rabbi and as of 2012 will enter her 40th year in rabbinic service. Lynn is a storyteller, percussionist, klezmer dancer, author and peace activist with a specialization in multifaith activism, the arts of resistance and Palestine solidarity work on behalf of a just resolution to the Israeli-Palestinian conflict. She has received several human rights awards, and her writing appears in more than 40 publications. Lynn is a member of the Fellowship of Reconciliation and currently works with FOR on the Peacewalk Project and Artist Delegations to Palestine. Lynn's book, *Trail Guide to the Torah of Nonviolence*, will be published by September 2012 in French and English. She currently performs a one-woman show called: "Pre-Occupied: Folktales and True Stories from the Holy Land."

Rabia Terri Harris

Chaplain Rabia Terri Harris is a teacher and student of transformational Islam. She founded the Muslim Peace Fellowship in 1994. As a contemporary theoretician of Islamic nonviolence, Rabia speaks and writes widely on issues of spirituality and politics. She has been engaged in interreligious education toward peace and justice for over 20 years, and is the beneficiary of over 30 years of traditional

Sufi education through the Jerrahi Order of America. A practicing Muslim chaplain holding credentials from Hartford Seminary and the Association for Clinical Pastoral Education, Rabia serves as president of the Association of Muslim Chaplains. She holds a BA from Princeton in Religion and an MA from Columbia in Middle Eastern Languages and Cultures, and works as an Adjunct Professor of Intellectual Heritage at Temple University. She is a scholar in residence at the Community of Living Traditions at Stony Point: (http://communityoflivingtraditions.org).

Ken Sehested

Rev. Ken Sehested, author of *In the Land of the Living: Prayers personal and public,* is co-pastor of Circle of Mercy in Asheville, NC. He was the founding director in 1984 of the Baptist Peace Fellowship of North America, a position he held until 2002. A graduate of New York University and Union Theological Seminary (NY), his work has taken him to more than 20 countries on every continent as a speaker, journalist and conflict mediator. Among his awards are the Dahlberg Peace Award of the American Baptist Churches USA, and a plaque of recognition for human rights advocacy in Latin America by the 2006 *Segundo Encuentro* of Baptist theologians in the Caribbean and Latin America. An award-winning author, his writing and poetry have appeared in more than two dozen magazines and books. Following three years of discussion, his congregation recently approved its own statement, "Circle of Mercy is a Peace Church," available at this link: http://sites.google.com/site/circleofmercy/Home/peace-church-statement.

Shomer Shalom Network for Jewish Nonviolence is a movement within Judaism dedicated to reconsecrating the Torah of Nonviolence. As it is written, "The entire Torah for the sake of peace" (Tanhuma Shoftim 18). Through the study and practice of nonviolent conflict transformation within rabbinic Judaism and contemporary anti-oppression work, Shomer Shalom seeks the spiritual resilience, creativity and skills needed for a lifetime pursuing active nonviolence. We offer study and prayer retreats, training programs, delegation experiences and a wide range of resources for individuals and groups interested in deepening their understanding of Jewish nonviolence. In addition, we provide an ordination program for rabbis, cantors and Jewish individuals who want to ground their expression of Judaism in the principles and practices of Jewish nonviolence.

> Shomer Shalom Network for Jewish Nonviolence
> Lynn Gottlieb, coordinator
> http://shomershalom.org/
> shomershalom@gmail.com • 805.259.503

The Baptist Peace Fellowship of North America gathers, equips and mobilizes Baptists to build a culture of peace rooted in justice. The BPFNA celebrates and supports peace work done by Baptist churches in North America by raising the visibility of these efforts through our publications and web site, by bringing peacemakers together in regional and international gatherings, and by providing resource, speakers and trainings. The BPFNA also actively connects with peacemakers from other traditions to build alliances and to work together toward our common goal of a more just and peaceful world. Learn more on our website or join our conversation on Facebook.

Baptist Peace Fellowship of North America
LeDayne McLeese Polaski, Executive Director
bpfna.org • bpfna@bpfna.org • 704.521.6051

Muslim Peace Fellowship/Ansâr as-Salâm was the first Muslim organization to be specifically devoted to the theory and practice of Islamic nonviolence. We understand unarmed struggle in pursuit of wise, just and compassionate social transformation to be the original and enduring genius of the Prophetic jihad. Part membership group and part think tank, MPF describes itself as "a gathering of peace and justice-oriented Muslims of all backgrounds who are dedicated to making the beauty of Islam evident in the world." You can learn more about MPF at our website or join our conversation on Facebook.

Muslim Peace Fellowship
Rabia Terri Harris, founder
www.muslimpeacefellowship.org
mpfrth@gmail.com • 845.786.5149

The Fellowship of Reconciliation seeks to replace violence, war, racism, and economic injustice with nonviolence, peace, and justice. FOR is an interfaith organization committed to active nonviolence as a way to transform life and as a means of radical change. We educate, train, build coalitions, and engage in nonviolent and compassionate actions locally, nationally, and globally.

Fellowship of Reconciliation
Mark Johnson, executive director
http://forusa.org/
for@forusa.org • 845.358.4601

building a culture of peace

of peace

www.ingramcontent.com/pod-product-compliance
Lightning Source LLC
Chambersburg PA
CBHW060310100426
42812CB00003B/730